HUNTING

JULIE K. LUNDGREN

ROURKE PUBLISHING

Vero Beach, Florida 32964

www.rourkepublishing.com

Photo credits: Cover © Blue Door Publishing; Title Page © Ivan Montero Martinez; Page 4 © Jeff Banke; Page 5 © John Wollwerth; Page 6 © Ivan Montero Martinez; Page 7 © GTibbetts, Vadim Kozlovsky; Page 8 © Crystal Kirk; Page 9 © Bodil1955; Page 11 © Bruce MacQueen, Vladi; Page 12 © Indigo Fish; Page 13 © Troy Kellogg; Page 14 © Blue Door Publishing; Page 17 © Tony Campbell; Page 18 © Sparkling Moments Photography; Page 19 © Danilo Ducak; Page 20 © SAMIphoto; Page 21 © Jeff Banke; Page 22 © Pedro Jorge Henriques Monteiro

Editor: Meg Greve

Project Assistance:
The author also thanks Julene Donnay, Andy Peterson,

Cover and page design by Nicola Stratford, Blue Door Publishing

Library of Congress Cataloging-in-Publication Data

Lundgren, Julie K.
  Hunting / Julie Lundgren.
     p. cm. -- (Outdoor adventures)
  Includes index.
  ISBN 978-1-60694-368-7
  1. Hunting--Juvenile literature. I. Title.
  SK35.5.L86 2010
  799.2--dc22

                                      2009008766

Printed in the USA

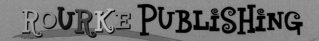

www.rourkepublishing.com - rourke@rourkepublishing.com
Post Office Box 643328 Vero Beach, Florida 32964

CONTENTS

The Hunting Tradition 4

Weaponry 6

Homework 10

Safety and Responsibilities 14

The Hunt 18

Glossary 23

Index 24

THE HUNTING TRADITION

People have hunted animals throughout human history. People today hunt for many reasons. The satisfaction of providing food for the table, the challenge and excitement of the chase, and family tradition bring new hunters to the sport every year.

Landowners who like to hunt often try to improve the **habitat** on their land so more animals or larger animals can live there successfully.

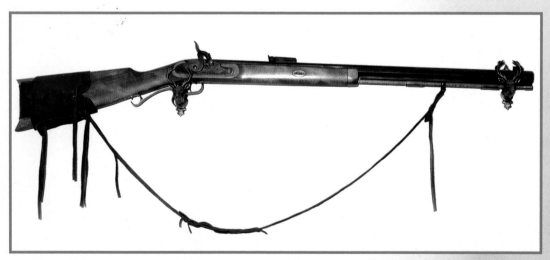

Hunters pack muzzleloaders with gunpowder, a little piece of cloth or paper, and a metal ball or shot through the tip of the gun known as the muzzle.

Early Americans used a kind of gun called a muzzleloader. Muzzleloaders are once again gaining in popularity.

WEAPONRY

Hunters match the weapon to the animal they are hunting and the hunting **season**. Rifles, each made for a specific size of **ammunition**, are commonly used for hunting many kinds of animals. Hunters use larger ammunition for deer, bear, elk, and other large animals. They use smaller ammunition for small **game** like rabbits and squirrels. Bird hunters favor shotguns. They must hit a small, speedy target.

Rifles shoot bullets with great accuracy over a long distance. Shotguns fire a shell filled with small metal pellets, called shot, over short distances. Hunters also use **slugs** in shotguns. Slugs make the shotgun perform more like a rifle and can be used on large game.

Shotgun shells have numbers printed on the side. The smaller the number, the larger the pellets inside.

sight   barrel   chamber

muzzle

action

guard

trigger

stock

Using a bow and arrow offers the hunter a special challenge. Because bows shoot shorter distances than guns, bowhunters must be much closer to the target animal. Wild animals frighten easily. Bowhunters need to use all their patience and skills to remain quiet, unseen, steady, and focused on the shot.

Bows come in different styles and sizes. Traditional **archers** may use longbows, recurve bows, or other styles. Other hunters prefer compound bows, which allow the user to fire arrows greater distances with more power. Compound bows, because they have many moving parts, can fail more often than simpler traditional bows.

Recurve bows have limbs that curve away from the user at their tips, while compound bows use a system of wheels and strings.

Unlike guns, which use gunpowder for power, bowhunters provide power for shooting arrows by bending the arms, or limbs, of the bow.

HOMEWORK

Successful hunters learn as much as they can about their **quarry**. They study the kind of habitat it prefers and how the animal meets its needs for daily living. They look for animal **signs**. This includes the tracks, trails, and other evidence that show the animal lives there. Knowing the animal helps hunters locate them in the field.

Know the laws that apply to the **harvest** of the target animal. Rule books say how many can be taken, the time of day and year, and what kind. The laws about **licenses** and youth hunting differ from state to state. Check with your state's fish and wildlife department to learn more.

TOP TIP

Animal feet sink into the snow and soft mud, making their tracks easier to see and follow.

TOP TIP

Practice shooting targets at different distances while standing, sitting, and lying down. This will increase your ability to hit your targets and learn your limits.

Well before the season starts, many hunters scout the land. They search for animal watering and feeding areas, animal tracks and trails, and rest places. They also look for the sneakiest places to enter the hunting area. Hunted animals learn where to expect trouble and stay away from those places.

Not everyone owns good hunting land. **Public land** offers opportunities for everyone. Public land managers can provide maps and share advice that gets hunters off to a good start.

Hunters wishing to hunt on private land should get permission from the landowner.

SAFETY AND RESPONSIBILITIES

Hunters must hunt safely and responsibly. Many states offer firearms and bowhunting safety training. They teach everything from hunting and shooting skills to hunting laws and survival skills.

Adult hunters gladly share their hunting knowledge with young people.

<u>The top safety rules for guns include the following:</u>

- Always treat a gun as if it is loaded with ammunition and could fire at any time.

- Keep the **safety** on and your finger off the trigger until just before shooting.

- Never point a weapon at anything you do not want to shoot.

- Be sure of your target and the location of your hunting partners.

- Unload the gun before climbing a tree or crossing a fence or stream.

- Unload the gun before placing it in a vehicle.

Bowhunters need to follow many safety rules, too. Among them, use caution when handling and carrying arrows, never shoot an arrow straight up into the air, and never climb while carrying your weapon.

Hunters have a responsibility to respect others and nature. The best hunters honor game animals and the sport by not littering, taking only the animals they will eat or use, and avoiding practices that do not allow animals a fair chance.

Since an arrow will not fly as far as a bullet, bowhunters often have an easier time getting permission from landowners to hunt on their land.

TOP TIP

Respect those who choose not to hunt by placing your game out of sight under a cover or in the trunk of your vehicle.

Hunting for trophy animals requires extra preparation. Trophies tend to be older, smarter animals with lots of experience avoiding hunters.

THE HUNT

Hunters dress carefully for the weather and the kind of hunt. Bowhunters and duck hunters often dress in **camouflage** clothing, while others rely on the safety of blaze orange, an extremely bright color that allows them to be seen easily by other hunters.

Camouflage clothing allows hunters to blend in with their surroundings.

White-tailed deer hunters often wait patiently on a raised platform called a stand.

The large, open lands of the western United States make it difficult for hunters to sit and wait for large game like mule deer. Hunters there prefer to spot animals from great distances using binoculars, and then move in just close enough to shoot.

Duck, turkey, and deer hunters sometimes use **calls** to locate a target animal or bring it closer. Once an animal moves into shooting distance, the hunter shoots. To avoid animal suffering, hunters only take shots they think they can make. If they wound an animal, they take responsibility for finishing the kill. Immediately after the kill, hunters often remove the animal's guts to allow the body to cool more quickly and avoid spoiled meat. It also makes the animal lighter to carry.

Some calls work by blowing through them.

Laws sometimes allow the use of animal models, called decoys, to bring game within shooting distance of the hunter.

Hunters love their sport and want to help take care of the land and its animals. Hunting clubs and organizations teach others about hunting and creating good animal habitats. Hunters and other nature lovers can then enjoy wildlife and continue the hunting tradition for many years to come.

Glossary

ammunition (am-yu-NIH-shun): bullets or shot loaded into a weapon

archers (AR-cherz): people who use bows and arrows, for either hunting or target competition

calls (KAHLZ): tools that hunters use to sound like the kind of animal being hunted

camouflage (KAM-uh-flahzh): coloring or shape that allows someone or something to blend in with its surroundings

game (GAYM): animals hunted for sport or food

habitat (HAB-uh-tat): an animal's natural home, which provides for all its needs

harvest (HAR-vehst): the killing of animals for human use

licenses (LYE-sehn-sehz): permits sold to someone so they can do an activity, like hunting and fishing

public land (PUHB-lick LAND): land open for use by all the people of an area, often managed by a government agency

quarry (KWOR-ee): the animal or prey that a hunter seeks

safety (SAYF-tee): a device on a firearm that locks the trigger so the gun cannot fire

season (SEE-zuhn): a period of time when hunting certain animals with certain weapons is allowed by law

signs (SINEZ): evidence an animal has left behind, such as tracks, waste, scratches on the ground or on trees, and nibbled plants

slugs (SLUHGZ): single lumps of metal that act as bullets for shotguns

Index

bird 6
bow(s) 8, 9
bullet(s) 6, 16
calls 20
clothing 18
decoys 21
deer 6, 19, 20
gunpowder 4, 9
habitat(s) 4, 10, 22
land(s) 4, 13, 19, 22

laws 10, 14, 21
muzzleloader(s) 4, 5
rifle(s) 6
safety 14, 15, 18
shotgun(s) 6
tracks 10, 11, 13

Websites

www.ducks.org/
www.bear-tracker.com/
www.fws.gov/
www.nssf.org/hunting/index.cfm?AoI=hunting
www.recreation.gov/

About The Author

Julie K. Lundgren grew up near Lake Superior where she reveled in mucking about in the woods, picking berries, and expanding her rock collection. Her interest in nature led her to a degree in biology. She currently lives in Minnesota with her husband and two sons.